The battle of Inkerman, 5th November 1854. A Russian attack on the British base was repulsed. The battle was fought in a fog so that a co-ordinated command of the soldiers engaged was impossible. The day consisted of a series of many individual encounters when the fighting spirit and skill at arms of the British carried them through to victory. The Russians suffered heavy losses and Inkerman was the Victorian soldier's greatest achievement.

THE VICTORIAN SOLDIER

David Nalson

Shire Publications

Contents

For Wendy Nalson

ACKNOWLEDGEMENTS

The author wishes to thank the following: Richard Eccles and Peter Tinker for permission to reproduce pictures of the soldiers and blockhouse on the Veldt (pages 15, top; 16, top); the Royal Logistic Corps Museum for the picture of Ladysmith, January 1900 (page 28, bottom); and Wendy Nalson for the maps (pages 12; 15, bottom; 17) and photographs of medals (pages 13, top; 16, bottom). All other illustrations are reproduced by permission of the Scarlet Gunner, 127 High Street, Tenterden, Kent TN30 6JS. The author is also obliged to the Victorian Military Society and its *Journal*, care of its Publicity Officer, 20 Priory Road, Newbury, Berkshire RG14 7QN.

Cover: *The 57th Foot, Duke of Cambridge's Own (the Middlesex Regiment), about 1895. This regiment was nicknamed 'the Diehards' after their badly wounded colonel called out 'Die hard, my men, die hard!' at the battle of Albuera in 1811, where they lost 423 men out of 570 engaged. Regimental traditions and individual characters played a big part in the Victorian army. The Duke of Cambridge was commander-in-chief of the British army between 1856 and 1895.*

British Library Cataloguing in Publication Data: Nalson, David. The Victorian soldier. – (Shire album; 352) 1. Great Britain. Army – Military life – History – 19th century 2. Great Britain. Army – History – 19th century 3. Soldiers – Great Britain – Social conditions I. Title 355.1'0941'09034 ISBN 0 7478 0460 5.

Published in 2000 by Shire Publications Ltd, Cromwell House, Church Street, Princes Risborough, Buckinghamshire HP27 9AA, UK. (Website: www.shirebooks.co.uk)
Copyright © 2000 by David Nalson. First published 2000. Shire Album 352. ISBN 0 7478 0460 5.
David Nalson is hereby identified as the author of this work in accordance with Section 77 of the Copyright, Designs and Patents Act 1988.
Printed in Great Britain by CIT Printing Services Ltd, Press Buildings, Merlins Bridge, Haverfordwest, Pembrokeshire SA61 1XF.

Life in Queen Victoria's army

During the reign of Queen Victoria (1837–1901) many changes occurred but life in 1901 was still vastly different from that in 2000. The living conditions of the middle and working classes at the end of Queen Victoria's reign give us an overwhelming impression of deprivation: not only no computer or television, but no modern cooker or washing machine. Conditions were hard. However, if one goes back just over another 63 years, to the accession of Queen Victoria in 1837, the lives of very many working men were, in the words of Thomas Hobbes, 'nasty, brutish and short'. One economist claimed that 'millions were a doomed class…their constitution is unimprovable and their wrongs irremediable'. In 1890 soldiers and their families ate $1^1/_2$ pounds (675 grams) of bread and 1 pound (450 grams) of meat per person per day, which was far more than the majority of the civilian population normally enjoyed.

It is against this background that the life of a man in the Victorian army should be viewed. Throughout the nineteenth century the army and navy were exclusively male organisations. It is likely that the principal reason a man enlisted in the army in the early years of Queen Victoria's reign was because he was unemployed and needed support. Conditions in the army, whilst not encouraging, were often better than outside it, particularly for those from Ireland, who made up the majority of ordinary soldiers.

The private soldier in the middle years of Queen Victoria's reign had a daily deduction, from his pay of 1s 2d, of $3^1/_2$d for groceries, vegetables and food, except for a pound (450 grams) of bread and three-quarters of a pound (341 grams) of meat, which were provided free of charge. If he wished to supplement the regulation dry bread for breakfast and tea, the soldier could spend a further 4^1/2d daily in the canteen. In addition, the soldier was charged 1d for washing and would also have to pay for some articles of uniform, underwear and cleaning materials.

Barracks were long, draughty rooms with primitive sanitation. Fresh water had to be obtained from wells or tanks outside. A section of the barracks was screened off by a canvas sheet or blanket for the married men and their families. One married man per eight cavalrymen or twelve infantrymen was allowed. The wives helped with the cooking and sewing and their presence may have curbed the soldiers' habits of hard drinking and hard swearing.

The army was unpopular with civilians. During the years of economic distress following the end of the Napoleonic Wars, in the absence of a proper police force, troops were often called out to deal with civil disturbances. Better men did not join the army, and the recruits were drawn from the unfortunate and those of bad character. Nevertheless, in time, most of the men became good soldiers and it is hard to find examples of their actions which brought discredit on their country when overseas. Many officers believed that flogging was necessary to enforce discipline among the bad elements of society. Flogging in peacetime was abolished in 1868 and in war in 1880. In 1868 a system of fines for drunkenness was instituted and in the same year the highest number (13.7 per cent) of soldiers in Queen Victoria's reign was court-martialled.

Edward Cardwell, Secretary of State for War from 1868 to 1874, instituted a profound reorganisation of the army. Cardwell's reforms are the watershed of the Victorian army. Before them, the system of enlistment for life meant that there had never been a reserve of trained men, nor were those in command trained for their role. There were no annual manoeuvres and few of the generals in England had had any practice of commanding large bodies of troops. In 1853 manoeuvres for a division were held but these were not very satisfactory. Successive emergencies had been met by improvisations. The matter was compounded by the reorganisation of the Indian Army after the Mutiny of 1857–9. Cardwell made the colonial territories largely responsible for their own security, thus releasing overseas garrison troops for the army at home.

At the time of Cardwell's reforms the regular army contained 141 battalions of infantry, each with its own number, under a Commander-in-Chief. Cardwell divided the country into sixty-six brigade districts based on county boundaries. Within each

Left: *The 16th Lancers. There were thirty-one cavalry regiments from 1868 to 1914. The principal overseas garrisons were India, Egypt and South Africa. Efficiency was hindered by officers being too old when they obtained the command of regiments and staying in command for too long – sometimes ten years. A royal commission recommended in 1876 that all general officers should retire at seventy. The cavalry regiments generally attracted a better type of recruit than the infantry ones. Infantrymen regarded cavalrymen as having too high an opinion of themselves and there were frequent fights between the two in the garrison towns.*

Below: *As with all large organisations, the Victorian army had officers with different abilities. They ranged from Field Marshals Roberts, Wolseley and Kitchener to those of whom Wolseley wrote that, if they had been private soldiers, he did not think any colonel would have made them corporals. This picture is of an aristocrat, Captain Houston-French of The Life Guards, in the splendid uniform of a leading regiment. As with the law, politics and the civil service, many Victorian army officers were from the aristocracy. It is said that no officer of the Household Cavalry had been through the Staff College by 1900.*

district, regular and non-regular forces were organised around a regimental depot, which was the administrative headquarters and basic training centre. Infantry regiments were linked in pairs, for example, the 28th Foot and the 61st Foot became The Gloucestershire Regiment, and the 62nd Foot and the 99th Foot The Wiltshire Regiment, brigaded with two militia battalions and local volunteers. Cardwell stated that his aims were to rationalise military resources and encourage recruiting by concentrating on local association. Of the two regular battalions, one would serve abroad and the other would provide replacements for it. Despite criticism of some unhappy amalgamations, and sentimental grief at the loss of the old regimental numbers, this was a definite improvement and helped avoid the long-standing problem of battalions being under strength.

The reforms also introduced the

short-service system. Up to 1847, men enlisted for life and their service was ended only by age or infirmity. Short service of twelve years, six with the regular forces and six with the reserve, was substituted. This, too, contributed to the rise in enlistment in the army. The purchase of commissions was abolished by royal warrant in 1871, although the performance of some generals in the South African (Boer) War of 1899–1902 did not reflect much improvement on the standard of those in the Crimean War of 1854-6. The War Office Act, 1870, gave the Secretary of State for War supreme authority over the army, a situation that has endured even during the world wars of the twentieth century.

The Cardwell Scheme was a great improvement and was economical with both men and money. There was an outburst of hostility, not only towards the changes, but also because they had been introduced by a civilian. The territorial designations, such as The Lincolnshire Regiment for the 10th Foot and The Suffolk Regiment for the 12th Foot, came into effect in 1881 when Hugh Childers was Secretary of State for War.

When Queen Victoria ascended the throne, cannon had scarcely changed since the days of Queen Elizabeth I. In 1855 a British inventor, W. G. Armstrong, designed a rifled cannon loaded from the breech. Previously cannon had been smooth-bore and muzzle-loaders. Improvements in fuses, gun-carriages and high explosives followed and by the end of Queen Victoria's reign cannon were not very different from those of the Second World War. The Crimean War was the first major campaign in which muskets with grooved or rifled bores were used extensively. The Lee-Enfield rifle was issued by the 1890s and enabled a soldier to shoot much more accurately without giving away his position by clouds of smoke.

Throughout Queen Victoria's reign the lance, a 9 foot (2.7 metre) long medieval weapon, was carried by some British cavalry regiments and was used to great effect as late as the battle of Elandslaagte in 1899, by the 5th Lancers. In 1903 Lieutenant-General Dunham Massey asserted in a letter to *The Times* that: 'Both in moral and physical effect [the lance] is incomparably superior to the sword in all situations, except close mêlée.' All this when the extensive use of the machine-gun was not very far in the future! The importance attached to the bayonet declined after the First World War, but in infantry fighting at close quarters in the Victorian era the psychological effect of cold steel was still great. However, even then, cannon and rifles were far more deadly than lances and bayonets.

In spite of the Cardwell reforms and the improvements in weaponry, by 1899, when the South African War began, military exercises, many of which dated from the eighteenth century, focused on rigid line formations, firing in volleys and bayonet charges. For ten months of the year the soldier was occupied with parading, cleaning

The Martini-Henry rifle superseded the Snider in 1871. The Martini-Henry was loaded at the breech, sighted to 1000 yards (914 metres) and used black powder. It was a hammerless, single-loading rifle with a heavy bullet that gave a violent recoil. It had an ejector which was worked by a lever behind the trigger guard. The first rifle to have a bolt action was the Lee Metford, which was first issued in 1888, but the Martini-Henry continued in use. The Martini-Henry rifle was 4 feet 1½ inches long (1.23 metres) and weighed 9 pounds (4.1 kg). There was increasing efficiency in the rifles issued to British infantry during the second half of Queen Victoria's reign.

The Royal Field Artillery with a 15-pounder gun in the 1890s. In spite of its importance, as shown in the battle of Gujarat (1849) in the Second Sikh War, artillery developed slowly during the years 1837–1901. The main improvements up to 1881 were in ammunition. In the middle of the nineteenth century breech loading was introduced for lighter guns but, because of problems with breech sealing, this was abandoned in 1865 and not reintroduced until 1881. The South African (Boer) War of 1899–1902 gave a great stimulus to artillery development. It is said that in 1899 the British 15-pounders were outranged by the Boers' 75 mm field-guns by 1000 yards (914 metres).

his equipment, looking after his uniform, doing guard duties and in valet or clerking activities, leaving only two months for training.

Each month companies had to complete four-hundred-page returns, which entailed an enormous amount of form filling by officers and non-commissioned officers. There were social and sporting activities in great abundance but no General Staff. An Intelligence Division was maintained in the 1890s at a cost of £11,000 per annum, whereas in Germany the General Staff were spending £250,000 on this service.

Throughout Queen Victoria's reign, the Foot Guards performed the Sovereign's Birthday Parade in her honour. There were also the two great Queen's Jubilee processions through London in 1887 and 1897. On the second occasion an observer wrote, 'the eye was filled with splendour, but fresh splendour came crowding in on it'.

By 1901 all the great nations of Europe except Great Britain had conscription. Queen Victoria's governments never had to resort to making military service compulsory by law. Apart from the Crimean War, no campaign involving the Victorian army was waged against a large or highly trained army. In any case, compulsory service was politically impracticable, and as late as 1916, in the midst of a world war, it was not possible to bring this in without a resignation from the Cabinet.

Even after the Cardwell reforms there were still fewer than half a dozen promotions each year from the ranks of the Victorian army. There were formidable obstacles to overcome: if an intelligent NCO obtained a first class Certificate of Education he would be hard pressed to cover his living expenses without a private income to supplement his pay, and the social barriers were almost insuperable. All this shows what a marvellous achievement it was for William Robertson. He enlisted in the 16th Lancers in 1877, obtained a commission in the 3rd Dragoon Guards in 1888 and, by 1900, had reached the rank of lieutenant-colonel. He subsequently became the only man to rise all the way to be a field marshal and Chief of the Imperial General Staff.

'Reading the Notice Boards'. In the eighteenth century recruiting sergeants were reputed to enlist men to train as soldiers by pressing the 'King's shilling' upon them in public houses. By the end of Queen Victoria's reign the sergeants had to inform the potential recruit, in plausible terms, of the advantages to be gained from changing his civilian way of life to that of a soldier. These advantages were also advertised in the eye-catching posters displayed on notice boards.

From civilian to soldier. After going to the recruiting office, a man would be given a medical examination and asked various questions. These questions covered not only his name, birthplace, age, trade and place of residence for the last three years, but also whether he had been an apprentice, was married, had been sentenced to imprisonment, was already in the army or the Royal Navy, or if he had been rejected as unfit for such service. A false answer to some of these enquiries made a man liable to punishment.

After answering the questions and confirming that he was willing to serve in the army, the recruit took the oath of allegiance to the Queen, which also stated that he would obey all orders of the generals and officers set over him. A certificate was then signed by a magistrate or attesting officer that he had cautioned the recruit, taken care that the recruit understood each question, that his answer thereto had been duly entered as replied to and that the oath had been taken before the magistrate or attesting officer. The recruit then had to report himself to his place of joining.

Field Marshal Viscount Wolseley (1833–1913). Known as Britain's 'only general', Wolseley conducted a number of the small wars which ran through Queen Victoria's reign almost without intermission. He carried out successful campaigns in Canada (1870), West Africa (1873–4), Zululand (1879) and Egypt (1882) but was sent out too late to relieve Major-General Gordon at Khartoum in the Nile expedition of 1884–5. Caricatured in the Gilbert and Sullivan opera 'The Pirates of Penzance', Wolseley did a great deal to prepare the army for the battles of 1914–15.

Campaigns

In very nearly every year of Queen Victoria's long reign, some part of the army was engaged in a campaign. However, such was the number of regiments that there were usually long gaps between periods of active service. For example, The Lincolnshire Regiment, after fighting in India between 1846 and 1858, was engaged only in Perak (Malaya) in 1875–6 until the reconquest of the Sudan in 1898. The Cheshire Regiment fought in the Sind War of 1843 but, except in Burma, not again until the South African War of 1899–1902.

Most of the wars fought by the Victorian army were against the native peoples of Asia and Africa. The wars that do not fall into this category are the Crimean War of 1854–6 and the campaigns against the Boers in the two wars of 1880–1 and 1899–1902. It would be wrong to belittle the victories of the British soldiers against non-European foes as these were usually formidable fighting men such as the Ashantis and Zulus in Africa and the Sikhs and Pathans in India. In many campaigns the superiority of British weapons was offset by the enemy's superior knowledge of the terrain, better endurance in the climate and greater numbers. Most of the campaigns of the Victorian army before 1870 were in India. After 1870, apart from the almost continuous fighting on the North West Frontier, the majority of the wars occurred in Africa, culminating in the South African War, which brought the greatest number of casualties (over 100,000) and the biggest expense (more than £200 million) since the Napoleonic Wars at the beginning of the nineteenth century.

The Crimean War was the only campaign against a European power during the Victorian era. Britain and France were seriously concerned at the prospect of Russia taking Constantinople and gaining access to the Mediterranean through the decaying Turkish Empire. Russia and Turkey had frequently been at war and the defeat of a

Turkish naval squadron by Russian forces at Sinope in 1853 escalated war fever in Britain and France, who went to Turkey's aid. After some preliminary campaigning in the Balkans, the Allied forces invaded the Crimea with the object of capturing the Russian naval base at Sebastopol. It is said that the instructions for these actions were approved at a Cabinet meeting at which more than half the members were asleep!

The French and British forces landed on the north-west side of the Crimea at Calamita Bay and

Field Marshal Lord Raglan (1788–1855), commander-in-chief in the Crimean war until he died in office. He had not seen action since the battle of Waterloo in 1815 and was an aged aristocratic gentleman who, the Duke of Wellington considered, would die rather than tell a lie. Raglan maintained good relations with his allies but his badly expressed order led to the destruction of the Light Brigade at Balaclava and his victories at the Alma and Inkerman were won for him by his troops.

The Charge of the Light Brigade. The imprecise wording of Lord Raglan's order to the commander of his cavalry division, Lord Lucan, launched the Light Brigade on their disastrous charge at the battle of Balaclava on 25th October 1854. Lucan did not understand the order and Captain Nolan, who delivered it, was no help. Should Lucan have disobeyed the order of his superior officer in the midst of a battle? The British love of a heroic catastrophe and Lord Tennyson's poem have enabled the Light Brigade charge, which took less than half an hour, to become the best-known military action of Queen Victoria's reign.

advanced south on Sebastopol. The Russian army had taken up a strong position on the heights bordering the river Alma. A gallant advance saw the heights captured and the way opened to Sebastopol. However, owing to a lack of intelligence about the weakness of the city's defences, the Allies decided to march round Sebastopol and besiege it from the south. From this direction the invading forces had good harbours in their rear for the transport of their supplies but unfortunately the delay enabled the Russians to strengthen the fortifications and prolonged the war.

The Russian army was not in Sebastopol and twice launched major attacks on the British forces which were holding the exposed eastern wing of the Allied armies. At Balaclava, on 25th October 1854, the Heavy Brigade of the British Cavalry Division distinguished themselves by making a successful charge on a vastly superior number of Russian cavalry. The Light Brigade mistakenly charged Russian gun batteries and suffered heavy casualties. Out of 673 horsemen who took part in this charge only a third answered the first muster afterwards. The orders of the Commander-in-Chief, Lord Raglan, were badly expressed and Lord Lucan, commanding the Cavalry Division, misunderstood them. This was the action which inspired Tennyson's poem *The Charge of the Light Brigade*. In true British fashion, the Light Brigade's disaster is remembered, but the magnificent effort of the Heavy Brigade, like the gallant stand of the 'thin red line' of the 93rd Highlanders against an attack by the Russian cavalry, is forgotten.

In the next major Russian attack, at Inkerman, the Victorian soldier was at his best. A surprise dawn attack in fog and rain was beaten off by the skill, gallantry and endurance of the men – a real 'soldiers' battle'. British and French forces, less than 16,000 strong, defeated 55,000 Russian troops who were armed with over two hundred guns. Moreover, 5000 French troops did not come into action. No finer battle was ever fought by Queen Victoria's army.

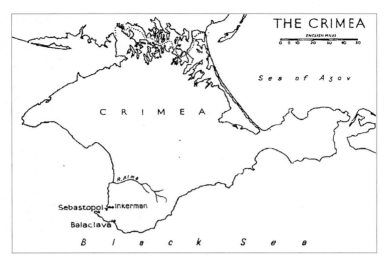

THE CRIMEA

In 1854 British maps of the Crimea were rudimentary. There was also little definite information on the Russian army. Yet the Allied army commanders hoped for a swift destruction of the naval base at Sebastopol followed by a speedy withdrawal. No attempt was made to seal off the Crimea from the rest of Russia, thus giving the enemy the opportunity to send reinforcements of men and supplies to their forces. Moreover, when Sebastopol was besieged, it was never completely surrounded and, by sinking ships across the harbour mouth, the Russians prevented the British and French fleets from carrying out a close-range bombardment from the sea. Florence Nightingale's hospital at Scutari was in Turkey on the other side of the Black Sea.

The fundamental mistake of the Crimean War was not capturing Sebastopol immediately after the victory at the Alma. Not only were the Russians, under the great engineer Todleben, given time to improve the fortifications, but the British army was condemned to spend the winter of 1854-5 conducting a siege. There was a lack of food, warm clothes, tents, huts and medical supplies. The troops suffered much from not having firewood, which meant they could not keep warm or cook. Cholera, malaria and dysentery raged among the siege lines, while supplies of the missing items were at Balaclava, about 5 miles (8 km) away. A light railway would have helped the situation considerably but the high command failed to organise matters.

The Crimean War was the first British campaign to be reported by a war correspondent. William Russell of *The Times* sent back details of the army's shortcomings. In 1855 his reports ignited a national agitation that helped bring about a change of government. Some of the worst muddles and mistakes were dealt with. Better weather brightened the Crimea and the assault on Sebastopol was set for 18th June 1855, the fortieth anniversary of the victory at Waterloo. The British were to attack the Redan. Unfortunately, Raglan and his aides sent the British forces to attack over a shell-swept approach of 450 yards (412 metres), an abattis and 20 foot (6 metre) wide ditch followed by an escarpment, with no preliminary bombardment. Furthermore, a very large proportion of the troops were young soldiers fresh from England. The British suffered a disastrous repulse. However, the Russians also lost heavily and it was said that their dead lay in 'heaps and heaps'.

Inevitably, another assault took place on Sebastopol on 8th September. The British attack on the Redan failed but the French captured the Malakof and the Russians evacuated the city. Threatened by an ultimatum from Austria, Russia agreed to a peace conference and in March 1856 the war ended. In addition to being noted for having the first war correspondent, the Crimean War also saw the foundations of

The Crimean War Medal was for service between 28th March 1854 and 30th March 1856. Two hundred and seventy-five thousand were awarded and there were five clasps or bars. The clasps are in the unique form of oak leaves and critics have complained that they resemble nameplates round bottles of whisky. Queen Victoria's head on this medal shows her much younger than that on the Queen's South Africa Medal (see page 16). The Crimean War Medal was awarded to some French forces. British, French and Sardinian troops were also awarded a medal by the Sultan of Turkey.

the army nursing system by Florence Nightingale, the earliest major war photographs and the institution of the Victoria Cross, a decoration open to all ranks.

Forty-three years after the end of the Crimean War, the Victorian army was confronted with its greatest test in the South African War – the Boer War. The Boer Republic of the Transvaal had been transformed by the discovery of gold on the Witwatersrand in 1886. The goldfields were developed by mainly British capital and labour. The Boer government refused to give the foreigners any political rights although they contributed about 95 per cent of the Transvaal's taxes. The Boers were also concerned about being almost encircled by British territories. After an abortive raid against the Transvaal by British South Africa Company forces, led by Doctor Leander Jameson, in 1895, war was inevitable.

At the start of the war, Boer forces invaded the British territories and besieged Ladysmith, Kimberley and Mafeking. An army corps was dispatched from Britain under Sir Redvers Buller and, as in 1914, it was widely thought that the war would be over by Christmas. On arriving in South Africa, Buller divided his force into three, sending Lord Methuen with one division to relieve Kimberley, Sir William Gatacre with another to defend the north-east of Cape Colony, while he himself

proceeded to Natal with the third to raise the siege of Ladysmith. Head-on attacks brought disaster. In the 'Black Week' of 10th–15th December 1899 Gatacre was defeated at Stormberg, Methuen at Magersfontein and Buller at Colenso. The losses of three thousand men in Black Week, although minute compared to

Field Marshal Earl Roberts (1832–1914). The son of a general, he won the Victoria Cross in the Indian Mutiny and served most of his career in India. Roberts was Commander-in-Chief in South Africa in 1900 during the period of British victories in the Boer War. During the war Roberts won many honours, including an earldom and the Order of the Garter, but lost his only son in action. Roberts was not much over 5 feet (1.52 metres) tall. He made great attempts to improve marksmanship in the infantry and artillery and was instrumental in establishing a club or similar institute in many British regiments in India.

Paardeberg (1900) was a major victory in the Boer War. General Cronje with over four thousand Transvaalers and Orange Free Staters surrendered to Lord Roberts. Ironically, Roberts himself had seriously considered retreating prior to the Boers' giving up. Cronje had occupied a strong defensive position on the north bank of the Modder river but was encumbered with women, children and wagons. The loss of oxen and horses destroyed the Boers' mobility and morale. Later, Lord Kitchener was to complain that the Boers did not stand up to a fair fight but were always running away on their ponies.

those of battles in the First World War, were followed by Buller signalling to Sir George White, the commander at Ladysmith, to fire away as much ammunition as he could and make the best terms with the enemy as possible. White, to his credit, declined to comply with this signal.

Black Week led to further reinforcements being sent out so that almost every regiment in the army was involved in the war. In addition, Lord Roberts replaced Buller as commander of the forces in South Africa, with Lord Kitchener as second in command. Buller became commander of the forces in Natal and persevered with the Ladysmith relief operations, being defeated again at Spion Kop and Vaal Kranz.

Roberts with his large army advanced on the Boer capitals of Bloemfontein and Pretoria. General French and a cavalry force were detached to relieve Kimberley, which was accomplished on 15th February 1900. The besieging Boer army under Cronje was surrounded at Paardeberg. The soldiers were kept busy digging trenches night and day, mostly under fire. Rations could only be brought up after dark and, added to lack of sleep, some troops were reduced to a half or a quarter ration of biscuit. Furthermore, it rained frequently. Nevertheless, Cronje was bombarded into surrender and by 5th June Roberts had captured Bloemfontein, Johannesburg and Pretoria.

The difficulties on the long marches involved were extreme. The Lincolnshire Regiment, for example, was issued with three-quarter rations on 18th February but from then to its arrival at Bloemfontein on 22nd March never more than a half ration with a third grocery ration was given out. Water was scarce and often very bad. Rains flooded the camps. Meanwhile, Buller had finally entered Ladysmith, and Mafeking, after a gallant defence for 217 days under Colonel Baden-Powell, was also relieved. To the British public and Roberts, it seemed that the war was over. In the circumstances at the time this was not unreasonable and if the Boer guerrilla leader, De Wet, had been captured, as he nearly was at Brandwater Basin, then hostilities could well have ceased. However, what followed was nearly two years of counter-insurgency operations under Kitchener, who succeeded to the supreme command when Roberts returned home in November 1900.

Not only were the Boers fighting in plain clothes, but their commandos were fed

During 1901 and 1902 the courage and endurance of the British soldier stand out. A vast country and an elusive foe must have made the long guerrilla phase of the Boer War seem unrelenting and unending. The army carried out exhausting drives, hampered by difficulties with supplies, especially forage for the horses, which affected the mobility of the forces. There was a constant problem with the supply of remounts, exacerbated by the wastage involved in ill-organised depots and half-trained riders on unacclimatised horses. Every captured British soldier provided the Boers with an efficient Lee-Enfield rifle and ammunition. It could be said that the enemy was rearmed with modern weapons at the expense of the British taxpayer.

The landlocked Boer Republics of the Transvaal and the Orange Free State might have used their resources to better effect in October 1899 by capturing Durban and so obtaining direct access to the outside world. Instead they besieged Ladysmith but never captured it. The size of the country greatly hindered the British army's attempts to capture the Boer guerrillas and end the war. Later conflicts such as the USSR's campaign in Afghanistan in the 1980s show that, even with sophisticated equipment, counter-insurgency operations are extremely difficult.

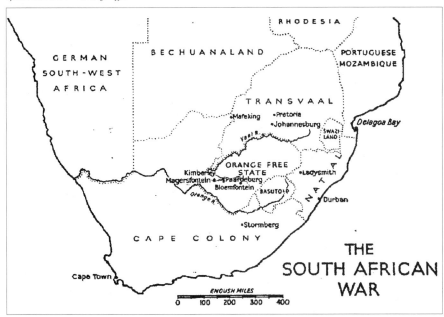

When the Boers adopted guerrilla warfare and avoided pitched battles, in which the British army had the advantage of greater numbers, a different strategy was called for. This involved erecting barbed-wire fences across the South African veldt, with miniature forts known as blockhouses at intervals. The blockhouses were constructed of concrete and tin and took advantage of the Boers' lack of heavy artillery. By 1902 there were over eight thousand blockhouses, covering 3700 miles (about 6000 km), supported by more than 65,000 troops.

The Queen's South Africa Medal was issued for the Boer War to: soldiers who served in South Africa between 11th October 1899 and 31st May 1902; troops in Cape Colony and Natal at the outbreak of hostilities; and those who guarded Boer prisoners at St Helena between 14th April 1900 and 31st May 1902. The reverse of the medal is shown here. There were twenty-six clasps, the most for any Victorian campaign medal. The rarest is that for the 'Defence of Mafeking'. Clasps were issued for service in Cape Colony, Natal, Orange Free State, Transvaal and Rhodesia as the vast number of small actions made it impossible to give a clasp for each one.

by the civilian population. Hence, Kitchener ordered farms to be burnt and women and children to be taken into concentration camps. The camps were often badly sited and usually inefficiently run, leading to the deaths of over 20,000 Boer women and children. The outcry this provoked was international and the bitterness long-lasting. A British lady, Miss Emily Hobhouse, denounced the camps and Sir Henry Campbell-Bannerman, leader of the Liberal opposition in the House of Commons, railed against the 'methods of barbarism' used in South Africa. The camps were handed over to civilian control while the hard-pressed military authorities got on with the war. The South African veldt was divided up with barbed-wire fences supported at intervals by blockhouses manned by troops, and this strategy led to the end of the conflict, marked by the Treaty of Vereeniging on 31st May 1902. The British army had secured South Africa for the Empire and as an ally in both world wars of the twentieth century.

India

In 1837 the chief authority in India was the Honourable East India Company, which had originally been a trading organisation but had become, through force of circumstances, a governing body. It had a court of directors in London and three armies in India, centred on the presidencies of Bengal, Bombay and Madras. The HEIC forces were composed mainly of Indians with British officers, although there were some wholly European regiments. In addition, British army regiments were hired from the crown.

In India in the 1840s it was reckoned that there were ten followers to every fighting man. The followers comprised men, women and children, about half of whom were simply hangers-on, usually there for what they could pick up. It was said that when Sir Charles Napier went on tour with fewer followers, because he had reduced the number of water-carriers by half, it was clear he did not wash!

Apart from the fighting in India, there were the heat, the flies, the mosquitoes and the risk of illness. Even after the Suez Canal began to be used for the Indian trooping service during the winter of 1868–9, the sea voyage from Portsmouth to Bombay still took over five weeks. Barrack accommodation was not available for all the troops and the punkahs, the fans which helped to cool down barracks, were not present in the tents which housed the remainder. Life in an overcrowded tent in the hot weather was exceedingly hard.

The victories of the Victorian forces in India are rendered more impressive when the primitive medical arrangements are considered. Moreover, little was known about diet and drink. The soldiers were not dressed for the climate at the start of Queen Victoria's reign and there was no air-conditioning. Hill-stations were considered more healthy than the plains but even there outbreaks of cholera occurred.

INDIA IN 1857

To the British private soldier, who usually had not travelled far from his place of birth, India must have seemed immense. The climate would have been a severe trial. In the plains, the heat from about 6 a.m. to 6 p.m. between April and November made any activity very difficult. Officers and men had to rise at 4.30 a.m. to get any work done. Some men were driven mad by the baking sun. The comparatively small area involved in the Indian Mutiny is evident from this map. The bulk of the Bengal army was recruited from Oudh. They were good soldiers but difficult to handle as many were of high caste.

17

Cholera, dysentery and a variety of stomach complaints caused havoc. Life expectancy could be very short. The lengthy sick-lists during the Burma campaign of 1942–5 and the morale-sapping effects of tropical campaigning experienced by the US army in Vietnam in the 1960s provide comparisons with the nineteenth-century campaigns of British troops, which are often overlooked but which show the calibre of the men of Queen Victoria's forces.

The pivotal event in British India during Queen Victoria's reign was the Indian Mutiny of 1857–9. It burst forth at Meerut in May 1857, ignited by the belief that the cartridges of the Enfield rifle were greased with cow and pig fat, thus defiling both Hindus and Muslims when they bit off the ends before loading. There were deeper causes, such as the prohibition of native customs, the age and ineffectiveness of senior officers, and the shattering of the aura of British invincibility by the catastrophic retreat from Kabul in 1842. Moreover, in 1857, there were 257,000 Indian troops and only 34,000 British in the country. The uprising involved the Bengal army but the Bombay and Madras armies were very largely unaffected.

The course of the Mutiny paralleled that of the Crimean and South African Wars, with problems in the earlier stages but a successful outcome. The mutineers from Meerut departed for Delhi and there was a failure to oppose them, which might have checked the spread of the Mutiny. On arriving at Delhi the rebellious sepoys sparked off a mutiny there. Further outbreaks took place at various centres including Lucknow and Cawnpore. At Lucknow, Sir Henry Lawrence, chief commissioner of

The blowing-up of the Kashmir Gate by a party led by Lieutenants Home and Salkeld began the storming of Delhi in September 1857. Several of the group were killed but this breach in the defences of the city led to its capture, which marked the turn of the tide in the Indian Mutiny. The Sikhs and the Gurkhas stayed loyal to the British in the great crisis and the Afghans did not invade in support of the rebels. Home, Salkeld, Sergeant Smith and Bugler Hawthorn were awarded the Victoria Cross for their gallantry. Over three thousand lives were lost at Delhi, more than in any other operation during the Mutiny.

Above: *The residency at Lucknow, which was defended by a British and Indian contingent under Sir Henry Lawrence from May to July 1857, and then under Colonel Inglis until the first relief in September of that year. However, the relievers were themselves besieged until Sir Colin Campbell effected a second relief in November. Campbell then withdrew the garrison from the residency and finally captured the city in March 1858. Unfortunately, the failure to prevent numerous mutineers escaping from Lucknow meant that they were able to offer resistance in Oudh for a further year.*

Right: *Field Marshal Colin Campbell, Lord Clyde (1792–1863) was, unusually for a Victorian general, of humble origins. Commander-in-Chief in India, 1857–60, during which time the Mutiny was suppressed, Campbell was one of the Victorian army's finest generals, whose campaign service stretched from the Napoleonic Wars at the beginning of the nineteenth century to the Crimean War and the Indian Mutiny. It is said that, when asked in 1857 how soon he could leave for India, he replied that, if he could be given half an hour to pack, he could be ready then.*

Oudh, fortified the residency, which held out for eighty-seven days until relieved. About half the force defending the residency was Indian. The residency itself was a group of houses without any specific perimeter about 400 yards (365 metres) by 200 yards (183 metres). An army, commanded by Generals Havelock and Outram, reached the residency on the 25th September 1857 but was itself besieged.

The British besieging force at Delhi was also invested on the ridge outside the city. The arrival of reinforcements from the Punjab enabled Delhi to be attacked on 14th September, when the Kashmir Gate was blown up, and, after a week of desperate street

The camp of exercise at Hassan Abdul in 1872. The exotic nature of soldiering in India lay not just in the mountains and jungles but also in the elephants and camels in regular use. The Royal Engineers calculated that a height of 15 feet (4.5 metres) and a width of 12 feet (3.6 metres) had to be allowed for the passage of a loaded elephant. On a good road, a loaded elephant advanced at $2\frac{1}{2}$ mph (4 km/h). This was also the speed of a loaded camel, but the height and width allowed for a camel were 11 feet (3.3 metres) and 10 feet (3 metres) respectively. Female elephants were preferred for military duties as they were more docile than males, and it was best to examine their feet carefully. The camels had to be properly fed to enable them to carry their loads.

Inspection of the 17th Bengal Infantry at Allahabad by General Roberts before their departure for Suakin. This was one of the occasions after the Indian Mutiny when Indian troops were used outside India. Suakin on the Red Sea was a British base for operations against the dervishes in the Sudan. Despite complaints from Indian authorities, the sub-continent provided a reservoir of trained manpower which could be extremely useful. Moreover, Indian troops were well able to stand the climate in places like Suakin. Money from the Indian treasury was also used towards the cost of overseas campaigns. £5000 was spent on the Sudan operations.

The King's Own Scottish Borderers in India, c.1890. By the last years of Queen Victoria's reign, the conditions in which the soldiers lived in India had improved. Flogging had been abolished, whereas, at the time of the Indian Mutiny, British troops were nicknamed 'bloody backs' by the sepoys from the prevalence of this punishment. Improvements had also been made in medicine, such as the discovery in 1883 that cholera was a water-borne disease. As can be seen in the picture, there had also been an increase in the firepower of British troops but the climate and terrain had still to be overcome.

The Bolan Pass. This pass, like the Khyber and the Kurram Passes, figured largely in the turbulent history of the North West Frontier of India. The area is inhabited by Pathans, who were probably the most ferocious people ever encountered by the Victorian soldier. Furthermore, there appeared to the British a very real threat of a Russian advance into India by this route. Two major wars were fought in Afghanistan, the buffer state between British and Russian spheres of influence, in 1838–42 and 1878–80.

fighting, the city was recaptured. The man who inspired the troops was Brigadier-General John Nicholson, who was killed in the attack. The taking of Delhi marked the end of the most dangerous phase of the Mutiny.

There had also been an outbreak of hostilities at Cawnpore, where the British surrendered after a siege lasting three weeks on being promised a safe conduct to Allahabad. Instead, the men were shot down and the women and children were imprisoned and later massacred, their bodies being thrown down a well. This was discovered when Cawnpore was retaken in December.

Troops under Commander-in-Chief Sir Colin Campbell fought their way through to the Lucknow residency, which was relieved on 17th November 1857. Campbell withdrew the garrison but had to leave the rebels holding the city. However, in March the next year he managed to capture it. Cawnpore had left an indelible memory and provoked acts of retribution, thus accounting for the slaughter of the mutineers in the Sikander Bagh at Lucknow.

Sir Hugh Rose carried out an efficient campaign in Central India in 1858. Of the rebel leaders, the Rani of Jhansi was killed by a trooper of the 8th Hussars and Tantia Topee was captured and hanged. Instigators of the Mutiny were blown from the guns. Gradually the disaffected areas were pacified during 1858 and 1859. In 1858 the Honourable East India Company was abolished and India, with the Indian Army, was taken over by the Crown. Most of the artillery was removed from native troops and there was an increase in the proportion of British forces in the sub-continent. British regiments in the Company's service were taken into the Queen's army.

After the suppression of the Indian Mutiny the main source of fighting in the sub-continent was the North West Frontier. However, it should not be assumed that the

The Punjab Frontier Force. By the last decade of Queen Victoria's reign it was apparent that the system of three separate presidential armies (Bombay, Bengal and Madras) was not suited for the defence of India. These armies were abolished in 1895 and replaced by four commands: Bombay, Bengal, Madras, and the Punjab, which last included the Punjab Frontier Force. Each command was under a lieutenant general responsible to the Commander-in-Chief in India, not to the governor of the presidency. The Punjab Frontier Force was maintained up to the early years of the twentieth century as a local force for the protection of the North West Frontier.

soldiers' time in India was spent on continuous active service or that ceremonial duties took up a disproportionate amount of their life. There were many opportunities for sport, which was encouraged as a vital part of a soldier's training. There were football, cricket, rugby, hockey, shooting and fishing. Many regiments spent a great deal of their time in India. In a host of ways it was a better life than the private soldier could hope for as a civilian in Great Britain. There were Indian servants to shave him and do his chores.

As in Great Britain, soldiers in India served their time against a changing background. In 1837 almost the only means of communication in India were the grand trunk routes of medieval days. By 1901 there was a network of roads, railways, canals and telegraphs. The lot of the soldier in India had also altered: there were improvements in cooking, sanitation, signalling, transport and the care of horses, and, following the example of Florence Nightingale in the Crimea, there was an Indian nursing service.

The impressive but impractical uniform of The Lincolnshire Regiment, 1897; a typical regiment of the line at this time. The spiked helmet was adopted from the Prussian army and was criticised for its design and its origin. Note the enormous amount of equipment carried. The uniform was thick and heavy, too. The brunt of all fighting in the Victorian era was borne by the infantry and, even after the advent of horse-drawn transport to move his heavier equipment, the infantryman had to carry himself most of what he needed. Speed of movement was a problem but this did not matter very much until the Boer War.

Uniforms

The uniforms of the Victorian soldier were many and various. What they were not, until quite late in the reign, was fitted for the work the soldier had to do. Although in India, from the time of the Mutiny of 1857 onwards, khaki clothing was used, red coats continued to be worn in action by the infantry up to the battle of Ginnis in 1885. At times there were military disasters: from the Retreat from Kabul in 1842 to Spion Kop in 1900, but the Victorian army always looked impressive.

Red had been the predominant military colour for British soldiers from the mid seventeenth century and was something to stir the blood. Another colour that was frequently used was blue, often indicative of a personal link with the sovereign. The more sinister colour black was seldom worn by British troops. A British soldier of an infantry regiment in 1840 would have worn a red coatee with white lace and a high collar, white duck trousers, white crossbelts, and a tall cap called a shako. The red coatee may have looked brilliant but it made a conspicuous target for the enemy, and the white trousers would obviously have been impractical. In 1845 the colour of the trousers was changed, as it was said that the constant washing required and the lack of proper drying facilities caused rheumatism. The crossbelts fulfilled a useful function as one held an ammunition pouch and the other a bayonet. In addition the soldier wore a large pack on his back. This was of blackened canvas with the regimental badge or number in the centre. On the pack the soldier carried a blanket and a mess-tin in a black oilskin cover.

By 1881 a soldier of a typical infantry regiment still wore a red coat both at home

Left: *The 1st Royal Dragoons. The helmet and the thick epaulettes served a useful purpose in deflecting some sword blows. However, the overall effect is of a conspicuous target. Most of the early Victorian fighting took place in India and cavalrymen such as this did not blend at all with their surroundings. Horses were a notable feature of the Victorian army and there was a series of spectacular charges – Aliwal in 1846, Balaclava in 1854, Ulundi in 1879, and Omdurman in 1898. The poor animals were to be involved in warfare for many years to come. It was said that cavalry raised the tone of what would otherwise have been a vulgar brawl, but no doubt the horses would have preferred to have avoided the brawl altogether.*

Below: *Uniform of the Scots Greys, a cavalry regiment. The rider wears a bearskin cap which is similar to that of the Foot Guards. His dazzling white crossbelt and gauntlets would take a vast amount of cleaning. The whole effect is of a 'toy soldier', and there is no indication that most of the Victorian cavalry's service was in the hot climates of India and Africa. The sole armament shown is a sword and the fighting power of this soldier is very limited.*

and on active service in Africa, but with no crossbelts, more practical blue trousers, and a spiked helmet. Since the successes of the Prussian army in the Austro-Prussian War of 1866 and the Franco-Prussian War of 1870, the British army had adopted the German headgear, although this was about the sum total of what it had assimilated. The coatee had been replaced by a tunic with a low collar. This was brought about not only by pressure of events, such as the soldier's increasing frustration at having to fight and march in unsuitable attire, but also by public opinion. The newspaper reports and photographs of the Crimean War made the general public more aware of the soldiers' problems. What may have seemed like a smart traditional uniform to old generals merely struck most ordinary people as restrictive and out of date.

The cavalry looked spectacular at all times and in all places up to nearly the end of Queen Victoria's reign. Helmets or thick hussar busbies were probably helpful in saving their

The uniforms shown here are reasonably practical if still coloured. One hopes the urgency shown in the picture was typical. The headgear contributes no useful purpose and the gunners would have been better off without it, wearing some sort of sunhat in hot climates. At least the artillery were taking part in cavalry manoeuvres: artillery manoeuvres with cavalry taking a subsidiary role was too much to expect!

wearer from sword cuts in action, but in general the uniforms were too tight, took up a disproportionate amount of time keeping them in order, and made the rider conspicuous. As one of the main duties of the cavalry was reconnaissance, a simpler uniform in a colour that would blend unobtrusively into the background would have been more effective. However, by the time the 21st Lancers made their celebrated charge at Omdurman in 1898 they were dressed in khaki for active service, although they still retained their spectacular full dress for ceremonial wear.

The first cavalry uniforms specifically designed for foreign service were the grey jackets with light brown breeches and white sun helmet worn by the camel detachment on the Gordon relief campaign of 1884–5. The white sun helmet had

The Camel Corps was formed from various cavalry regiments in the expedition that was despatched to rescue General Gordon from Khartoum in 1884. Although the forces were sent out too late to save the general, the formation of the Camel Corps represented an attempt to adapt to foreign circumstances. The Martini-Henry rifle is shown, which was a far better weapon than a sword or a lance. In another break with tradition, there was no scarlet in the uniform. Blue-lensed goggles were worn to offset the bright sunlight. The officers and men were also issued with water bottles.

been brought in for all soldiers on foreign service in 1877. Khaki, which is the Persian word for 'dust colour', originated in India. The British soldier of the early years of Queen Victoria's reign wore white clothing in India and this outfit was dyed using a variety of items such as curry powder and coffee to produce a khaki colour. Some regiments wore this during the Indian Mutiny. Afterwards, however, khaki fell into disuse and was not revived until the Second Afghan War of 1878–80. The Royal Artillery was dressed in blue for the majority of Queen Victoria's reign, changing to khaki for active service after 1885, so falling into line with the rest of the army.

In 1888 the Slade-Wallace equipment was introduced. The names were those of the designers and the equipment consisted of two pouches and two cross braces passing over the shoulder, and a waistbelt. There was a valise at the top of the

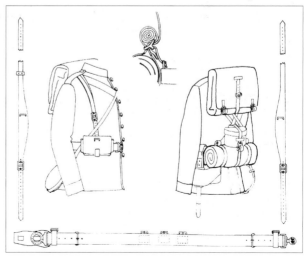

Valise equipment pattern, 1888. The Slade-Wallace equipment consisted of a waistbelt, which was adjustable at both ends, with brace attachments long enough to pass around a rolled greatcoat when necessary. The pouches had special internal fitments, which came to carry fifty rounds of ammunition, and slipped on to each side of the waistbelt. The valise of black japanned canvas was held by two straps that passed over the shoulders like the braces. All strappings were of white buff with brass fittings (or black leather with yellow fittings for the Rifles).

Left: *A sergeant and three privates. The three stripes on his sleeve denote the sergeant, otherwise his uniform is similar to that of the private soldier. The shine on the boots and the vivid whiteness of the belts are evidence of the hours spent on getting the outward appearance of the soldier up to the high standard deemed necessary. Ironically, at the end of the nineteenth century the army was to be severely tested by Boer forces of ineffable scruffiness. The prominence of the bayonet in this picture reflects how highly it was regarded by many contemporary general officers.*

Below: *A business-like group of soldiers at Ladysmith in January 1900, with hats to ward off the sun and uniforms to merge into the background. The authorities had had to bow to pressure by now. The equipment draped on the uniforms is kept to a minimum. The need for camouflage and rapid movement had been forced upon the British forces by the nature of the war in South Africa. The outfits worn by the British were still, however, homogeneous.*

The shako was the headgear of the majority of the army when Queen Victoria came to the throne in 1837 and was to remain so until the introduction of the spiked helmet after 1870. The shako had a number of variations but the basic pattern remained the same. It was a smart and practical piece of uniform and did not take a lot of time to clean and keep in order. A row of shakos looked like a castellated wall of a medieval fortress and added to the impressive appearance of the soldiers.

soldier's back and, underneath this, a mess-tin and rolled blanket, a development from the earlier pack of the 1840s.

Apart from Highland regiments, the head-dress generally worn by the majority of the army in Queen Victoria's reign was a shako up to the late 1870s and then the spiked helmet (which has continued to be used for bandsmen up to the present day). There were various types of shako. The 1869–78 pattern was made of stiffened blue cloth and had a black leather peak. The height was 4 inches (10 cm) at the front and $6^1/2$ inches (16.5 cm) at the back. It was kept in place by a chain, made of brass interlocking rings backed with leather, which went under the soldier's chin. The chain fitted to the shako on each side with rosettes. The spiked helmet was made of cork and covered with cloth. The peak was rounded and bound with leather. The top of the helmet had a crosspiece and the spike was attached to this. The spiked helmet was kept in place by a chain similar to that of the shako.

The white foreign service helmet was also made of cork but covered with white cloth. It was authorised in 1877 although it had been worn before then in India. This helmet was longer at the back, where it measured 12 inches (30 cm) from top to bottom, with the front measuring $10^3/4$ inches (27 cm). Sometimes a khaki cover was worn with the helmet and also a neck flap to keep off the sun's rays.

The colours of the uniforms were often a factor in the choice of nickname for a particular regiment. The Royal Horse Guards became known as 'the Blues', the 21st Lancers became 'the Grey Lancers' and the 5th Royal Irish Lancers 'the Redbreasts'. Whatever the regiment, one of the most striking features of Victorian uniforms that have survived is their small size. This is a graphic reminder that the men of a hundred years ago were much smaller than those of today.

The Victorian soldier may not have taken part in any world wars but he fought almost all over the globe and almost always successfully. He deserves to be remembered.

Further reading

Anglesey, the Marquess of (editor). *Sergeant Pearman's Memoirs.* Jonathan Cape, 1968.

Ascoli, David. *A Companion to the British Army.* Harrap, 1984.

Beaumont, Roger. *Sword of the Raj.* Bobs-Merrill, 1977.

Bonham-Carter, Victor. *Soldier True: The Life and Times of Sir William Robertson.* Frederick Muller, 1963.

Brighton, Terry. *The Last Charge: The 21st Lancers and the Battle of Omdurman.* The Crowood Press, 1998.

Carver, Lord. *The Seven Ages of the British Army.* Grafton Books, 1986.

Chandler, David G., and Beckett, Ian F. W. (editors). *The Oxford History of the British Army.* Oxford University Press, 1996.

Edwardes, Michael. *Battles of the Indian Mutiny.* Pan, 1970.

Ensor, R. C. K. *England 1870–1914.* Oxford University Press, 1936.

Ffrench-Blake, R. L. V. *A History of the 17th/21st Lancers.* Hamish Hamilton, 1968.

James, David. *Lord Roberts.* Hollis & Carter, 1954.

Jeal, Tim. *Baden-Powell.* Pimlico, 1991.

Keown-Boyd, Henry. *A Good Dusting.* Guild Publishing, 1986.

Lehmann, Joseph. *All Sir Garnet.* Jonathan Cape, 1964.

Longford, Elizabeth. *Wellington: Pillar of State.* Panther, 1975.

Lunt, James. *The Scarlet Lancers.* Leo Cooper, 1993.

Messenger, Charles. *History of the British Army.* Bison Books, 1986.

Pakenham, Thomas. *The Boer War.* Futura, 1988.

Pemberton, W. Baring. *Battles of the Crimean War.* Pan, 1968.

Pemberton, W. Baring. *Battles of the Boer War.* Pan, 1969.

Swinson, Arthur. *North-West Frontier.* Corgi, 1969.

Swinson, Arthur, and Scott, Donald (editors). *The Memoirs of Private Waterfield.* Cassell, 1968.

Wilkinson-Latham, R. and C. *Cavalry Uniforms.* Blandford Press, 1969.

Wilkinson-Latham, R. and C. *Infantry Uniforms 1742–1855.* Blandford Press, 1969.

Wilkinson-Latham, R. and C. *Infantry Uniforms 1855–1939.* Blandford Press, 1970.

Woodham-Smith, Cecil. *The Reason Why.* Penguin Books, 1958.

Woodward, Llewellyn. *The Age of Reform.* Oxford University Press, 1979.

Places to visit

Abington Museum, Abington Park, Northampton NN1 5LW. Telephone: 01604 631454.

Aldershot Military Museum, Queen's Avenue, Aldershot, Hampshire GU11 2LG. Telephone: 01252 314598.

The Argyll and Sutherland Highlanders Regimental Museum, The Castle, Stirling FK8 1EH. Telephone: 01786 475165. Website: www.argylls.co.uk

Army Medical Services Museum, Keogh Barracks, Ash Vale, Aldershot, Hampshire GU12 5RQ. Telephone: 01252 340212.

Army Physical Training Corps Museum, Army School of Physical Training, Fox Lines, Queen's Avenue, Aldershot, Hampshire GU11 2LB. Telephone: 01252 347168.

The Black Watch Regimental Museum, Balhousie Castle, Hay Street, Perth, Perthshire PH1 5HR. Telephone: 0131 310 8530.

Border Regiment and King's Own Royal Border Regiment Museum, Queen Mary's Tower, The Castle, Carlisle, Cumbria CA3 8UR. Telephone: 01228 532774.

British in India Museum, Newtown Street, Colne, Lancashire BB8 0JJ. Telephone: 01282 613129.

Cheshire Military Museum, The Castle, Chester, Cheshire CH1 2DN. Telephone: 01244 327617.

Coldstream Museum, 12 Market Square, Coldstream, Berwickshire TD12 4BD. Telephone: 01890 882630.

Doncaster Museum and Art Gallery, Chequer Road, Doncaster, South Yorkshire DN1 2AE. Telephone: 01302 734293.

Essex Regiment Museum, Oaklands Park, Moulsham Street, Chelmsford, Essex CM2 9AQ. Telephone: 01245 615100. Website: www.chelmsfordbc.gov.uk

Firepower, Royal Arsenal West, Warren Lane, London SE18 6ST. Telephone: 020 8855 7755. (Opens 2001.)

Fort Brockhurst, Gunner's Way, Elson, Gosport, Hampshire PO12 4DS. Telephone: 01705 581059. (English Heritage)

Fusiliers' Museum Lancaster, Wellington Barracks, Bolton Road, Bury, Lancashire BL8 2PL. Telephone: 0161 764 2208.

The Green Howards Museum, Trinity Church Square, Richmond, North Yorkshire DL10 4QN. Telephone: 01748 822133.

King's Own Regimental Museum, Market Square, Lancaster, Lancashire LA1 1HT. Telephone: 01524 64637. Website: www.lancaster.gov.uk/council/museums

Military Museum Bodmin, The Keep, Bodmin, Cornwall PL31 1EG. Telephone: 01208 72810.

Museum of Lincolnshire Life, Burton Road, Lincoln, Lincolnshire LN1 3LY. Telephone: 01522 528448.

Museum of The Manchester Regiment, Ashton Town Hall, Market Place, Ashton-under-Lyne, Lancashire OL6 6DL. Telephone: 0161 342 3078 or 342 3710. Website: www.tameside.gov.uk

National Army Museum, Royal Hospital Road, Chelsea, London SW3 4HT. Telephone: 020 7730 0717. Website: www.national-army-museum.ac.uk

The Queen's Royal Lancers Museum, Belvoir Castle, Belvoir, Grantham, Lincolnshire NG32 1PD. Telephone: 01159 573295.

Redcoats in the Wardrobe, 58 The Close, Salisbury, Wiltshire SP1 2EX. Telephone: 01722 414536. Website: www.thewardrobe.org.uk

Regimental Museum: 1st The Queen's Dragoon Guards, Cardiff Castle, Cardiff CF10 3RB. Telephone: 029 2022 2253.

Royal Armouries at Fort Nelson, Down End Road, Fareham, Hampshire PO17 6AN. Telephone: 01329 233734. Website: www.armouries.org.uk

Royal Armouries Museum, Royal Armouries, Armouries Drive, Leeds LS10 1LT. Telephone: 0113 220 1999 or 1916. Website: www.armouries.org.uk

Royal Engineers Museum, Prince Arthur Road, Gillingham, Kent ME4 4UG. Telephone: 01634 406397.

The defence of Rorke's Drift. The warlike kingdom of the Zulus appeared to be a major threat to the British colony of Natal and the Boers in the Transvaal, and a pre-emptive strike was launched in 1879. In the ensuing Zulu War, the camp of the central column of the British forces at Isandhlwana was overrun. This disaster was followed by the epic defence of the mission station at Rorke's Drift by B Company of the 2/24th Foot (South Wales Borderers) under Lieutenants Chard and Bromhead. Seven Victoria Crosses were won and a Zulu invasion of Natal was thwarted. The gallant action at Rorke's Drift made a greater impression on the Victorian public than Lord Chelmsford's victory at Ulundi which shattered the Zulu army.

The Royal Hampshire Regiment Museum, Serle's House, Southgate Street, Winchester, Hampshire SO23 9EG. Telephone: 01962 863658.

Royal Logistic Corps, Deepcut, Camberley, Surrey GU16 6RW. Telephone: 01252 340871.

Royal Norfolk Regimental Museum, Shirehall, Market Avenue, Norwich, Norfolk NR1 3JQ. Telephone: 01603 223649. Website: www.norfolk.gov.uk/tourism/museums/regi.htm

Shropshire Regimental Museum, The Castle, Shrewsbury, Shropshire SY1 2AT. Telephone: 01743 262292.

Somerset Military Museum, County Museum, Taunton Castle, Taunton, Somerset TA1 4AA. Telephone: 01823 320200. Website: www.somerset.gov.uk/museums

The South Wales Borderers and Monmouthshire Regimental Museum of the Royal Regiment of Wales, The Barracks, Brecon, Powys LD3 7EB. Telephone: 01874 613310. Website: www.rrw.org.uk

Staffordshire Regiment Museum, Whittington Barracks, Lichfield, Staffordshire WS14 9PY. Telephone: 0121 311 3229.

York and Lancaster Regimental Museum, Central Library and Arts Centre, Walker Place, Rotherham, South Yorkshire S65 1JH. Telephone: 01709 823635. Website: www.rotherham.gov.uk